This sticker books belongs to

oooooooooooooooooooooooooooooooooooooooooooo

oooooooooooooooooooooooooooooooooooooooooooo

Date started

oooooooooooooooooooooooooooooooooooooooooooooooooooooooooo

This book is filled with all the stickers
I have worked hard to earn
at oooooooooooooooooooooooooooooooooooooooooooooooo

oooooooooooooooooooooooooooooooooooooooooooooooooooooooooo

Date

Date

Date

Date

Date

Date

Date

Date

Date

Date

Date

Date

Date

Date

Date

Date

Date

Date

Date

Date

Date

Date

Date

Date

Date

Date

Date

Date

Date

Date

Date

Date

Date

Date

Date

Date

Date

Date

Date

Date

Date

Date

Date

Date

Date

Date

Date

Date

Date

Date

Date

Date

Date

Date

Date

Date

Date

Date

Date

Date

Date

Date

Date

Date

Date

Date

Date

Date

Date

Date

Date

Date

Date

Date

Date

Date

Date

Date

Date

Date

Date

Date

Date

Date

Date

Date

Date

Date

Date

Date

Date

Date

Date

Date

Date

Date

Date

Date

Date

Date

Date

Date

Date

Date

Date

Date

Date

Date

Date

Date

Date

Date

Date

Date

Date

Date

Date

Date

Date

Date

Date

Date

Date

Date

Date

Date

Date

Date

Date

Date

Date

Date

Date

Date

Date

Date

Date

Date

Date

Date

Date

Date

Date

Date

Date

Date

Date

Date

Date

Date

Date

Date

Date

Date

Date

Date

Date

Date

Date

Date

Date

Date

Date

Date

Date

Date

Date

Date

Date

Date

Date

Date

Date

Date

Date

Date

Date

Date

Date

Date

Date

Date

Date

Date

Date

Date

Date

Date

Date

Date

Date

Date

Date

Date

Date

Date

Date

Date

Date

Date

Date

Date

Date

Date

Date

Date

Date

Date

Date

Date

Date

Date

Date

Date

Date

Date

Date

Date

Date

Date

Date

Date

Date

Date

Date

Date

Date

Date

Date

Date

Date

Date

Date

Date

Date

Date

Date

Date

Date

Date

Date

Date

Date

Date

Date

Date

Date

Date

Date

Date

Date

Date

Date

Date

Date

Date

Date

Date

Date

Date

Date

Date

Date

Date

Date

Date

Date

Date

Date

Date

Date

Date

Date

Date

Date

Date

Date

Date

Date

Date

Date

Date

Date

Date

Date

Date

Date

Date

Date

Date

Date

Date

Date

Date

Date

Date

Date

Date

Date

Date

Date

Date

Date

Date

Date

Date

Date

Date

Date

Date

Date

Date

Date

Date

Date

Date

Date

Date

Date

Date

Date

Date

Date

Date

Date

Date

Date

Date

Date

Date

Date

Date

Date

Date

Date

Date

Date

Date

Date

Date

Date

Date

Date

Date

Date

Date

Date

Date

Date

Date

Date

Date

Date

Date

Date

Date

Date

Date

Date

Date

Date

Date

Date

Date

Date

Date

Date

Date

Date

Date

Date

Date

Date

Date

Date

Date

Date

Date

Date

Date

Date

Date

Date

Date

Date

Date

Date

Date

Date

Date

Date

Date

Date

Date

Date

Date

Date

Date

Date

Date

www.ingramcontent.com/pod-product-compliance
Lightning Source LLC
Chambersburg PA
CBHW051001060726
47593CB00018B/2266
* 9 7 8 1 7 9 7 0 9 8 6 7 8 *